I Want
A Poem
About
Kansas

by Susan Kinney-Riordan

HORIZONS
Impacting the Cultural Community in Salina since 1986
Salina Arts & Humanities Commission • City of Salina

East Window Press

2037 Roach
Salina, KS 67401

ISBN: 0-9755656-0-5
Library of Congress Control Number: 2004111197

Cover design by Pamela Harris, Salina, KS

In memory of my mother,
Mary Frances MacRae Kinney.
Thank you for returning me to my poetry.

CONTENTS

INTRODUCTION

Poetry saved my life. Without poetry, I would not have survived as a teenager or gotten through my parents' divorce. Poetry helped me when my mother had a heart attack. My poetry helped me stay sane while raising four kids. My poetry also brought me back from a stroke.

From 2000-2002, I worked on my master's degree in writing with a concentration in women's poetry. In that time, I wrote 150 poems. From those poems, I chose those that became my thesis project manuscript, and from that manuscript I chose the seventy-three poems that became this book.

The title originally was *The Muse Is Dead. She's Buried In Kansas.*

My professors in Vermont at the university I attended asked me to state what I was trying to prove with my thesis. I told them I wanted to prove that women poets use their surroundings to feed their imaginations rather than a muse. I had to add a qualifier to the thesis title to satisfy them: *The Muse is Dead. She's Buried in Kansas: The Landscape of a Woman Poet.*

The landscape of a woman is what these poems are about. They tell about my life. I could never write any other way. Poetry is a way for me to say the things that there are to say about my life. It is a way for me to witness to my life. My voice is a poetic voice. Even when I write other things, the poetry comes out.

Poetry is a part of my life. Without it I could not function.

Traveling Shoes

AFTER THE CHIEFTAINS CONCERT

Puddle lakes gather
in the fields,
headlights flash past.
Steering the black wheel,

Gaelic sounds that
rang the rafters
pound in your head.

Peering through the
dark curtain of rain
praying to saints,
pagan goddesses or
anyone who will listen.

An Irish chant
fades with the night.
Tread on the gas pedal.
Cars, trucks and signs
lead you home.

ALL CREATURES SEEK REFUGE

My path lit by
city lights as I
head for home
down the
four lane thoroughfare
lined with pizza
parlors and used
car lots.
A white tipped tail
connected to a fox
zips across
my car's path
in the evening
dusk. Into the trees
all creatures seek
their refuge.

BIRKENSTOCK CATALOG

I pore over it looking at shoes.
The catalog label
is addressed to my daughter.
Why? She ordered a pair of shoes.
Now maybe
I can get my shoes back.
But I sure do like the ones
called Pasadena.
Is Pasadena in California?
Yeah, she answers.
All she cares about is Prague.
Prague, of all places.
They are fighting over there,
aren't they?
People shot in the capital city,
a tire shot out that looks like Swiss cheese.
Prague isn't the problem.
A walk around your hometown
is the problem.
Who knows
what will happen
when you open the door.

NOT AT HOME

The small bedroom
off the lounge
with a kitchen. A home
not truly mine. But
for this week
I pore over books,
write in notebooks, listen
to speakers. A place
in the Vermont
woods on a hill
in what is called
The Green Mountains.
Home is far away
in Kansas.

GO TO INFINITY

Distances

From here to there

Miles to go

Even if it is only
to the doctor's office
or grocery store

A three block walk

Looking down the streets
that go to infinity

Going on is something
we do without thinking

FLINT HILLS TO COLORADO

The highway cuts
through their layered
surface as it moves
past cattle chewing
plains grass torn
from atop these
wash downed
mountains.
The road's gray
cement moves
to another set
of mountains.
Blue white coolness blows
in the open window.
Rockies loom
behind a city
as the highway
twists and turns
going up and up,
cows forgotten
in the climb.

CAR RIDE TO EAGLE NEST

The highway winds around
lodgepole pines
until it drops
into the bowl
of lake, buildings,
and brown grass
encircled by trees.

Overhead
its namesake flies
as we slide
to a stop.
Our stomachs churn
the grief
we hold inside.

ALL GOD'S CHILDREN NEED TRAVELING SHOES

Slip on beige suede clogs
tie brown oxfords
pull on rubberized boots.
My traveling shoes
take me down sidewalks
onto airplanes that fly
my wandering soul
to the next place.
The itch to be gone
drives my feet.

ANOTHER HORIZON

I long to go
just to see
islands
in tropical blue sea
and walk their perimeter.

Not like here
where sky is forever.
Over the next rise
more land.
Another horizon
going towards
always
going towards
another horizon.

I Wanted A Poem About Kansas

DIRT IN KANSAS

Dust blows
across a highway
from a newly tilled field.

Grit blows
on country roads
as cars and trucks
go back and forth.

Sand brought back
in shoes and towels
after swimming
at the lake.

Enough dirt wasted
to build a world.

I WANTED A POEM ABOUT KANSAS

Poem after poem
read and reread
saying oceans
and shells.
Saying mountains
and valleys.
No one says
flatlands and prairies
and small scurrying animals.
No one says who
lives there?
Who stands looking
far away
to mountains and oceans?

Say land of wheat.
Say the names of rivers—
Solomon, Smoky Hill,
Kansas, Marais des Cygnes.
Say towns and places
no one knows—
Concordia, Ellsworth,
Oskaloosa, Netawaka.
Say a life lived
on the plains.
Count the numbered years.
Say the shout of anger
to the mountains or ocean.
Only a whispered poem
in your ear.

ONE HUNDRED TWELVE DEGREES

Night flows over
a super heated body
awash with sweat.

Eyelids heavy.
Sleep comes tiptoeing
to a tune that purrs
in the hot
August night.

Night time ritual
recedes into reflection.
Breath caresses breast bone,
night slips into
its concealing, sweltering
black dress.

PICKING UP MY DAUGHTER FROM HORSEBACK RIDING LESSONS

> "paying attention to small beauties,
> . . . as if it were our duty . . ."
> —Sharon Olds, "Little Things"

I travel down a no outlet
minimum maintenance
sand covered road.
At the end two birds
begin a sedate stroll
across the road.
Then in view
I holler
wild turkeys
into the tall grass.
They flee.

Turning down the drive
I park and wait
window down
to let the evening air
blow through.
Horses whicker,
a jet goes over,
the county maintainer's truck
grinds its gears.
The quiet a gift
so close to the city.

THE MUSE IS DEAD. SHE'S BURIED IN KANSAS

I scan the horizon.
The outline of grain elevators against the sky
looks like gravestones.
Horizon and sky touchstones
for life lived on the prairie.

Traveling the highways
I watch and look.
Dry fields and soybean harvest.
Favorable weather
it says on the USDA paperwork.

Farming in Kansas a gamble
worthy of Las Vegas.
My father-in-law said,
"The only sure things
about farming in Kansas
is death and taxes."

WATCHING THE SKY

First it was pale white gray
then the dark charcoal of a dead fire.

Up above the thunder
rolls over. An orchestra's
timpani is the only instrument playing.
Sometimes it sprinkles, sometimes not
and the earth's dryness
soaks it in
trying to quench
its drought-caused thirst.

The wheat will sprout
and the farmer in my husband
will sigh with relief.
Another crop
another tractor
another year
for harvest.

TORNADO WARNING

Unstable cell they
call it as they watch
the radar screen.

Is the wind cloud
rotating? Dark energy
moving across the land,
pulling up grass,
leveling a pump house.

The sound comes and goes
as the radio spouts
words to describe.

No water for the citizens.
Tomorrow begins the
clean up.

A FLATLANDER NEEDS TO SEE THE SKY

Twisting down mountain roads
leaves a hole in my stomach.

Closed eyes as the
Jaguar zips around
our car too fast.

The prairie spreads out
below me solid,
strong, hard packed
as I move across it.

Flatlanders need to
see the sky.

THEY CROSSED AN OCEAN FOR KANSAS

An ocean and years apart
they walked to the horizon.

Looking beyond the
green that they carried
in trunks and Bibles.

Land that didn't
raise potatoes.

Land that belonged
only to them.

Land as far
as the eye could see.

They crossed an
ocean
for this.

MIGRATION

Traveling by ship
and oxcart
they made their
migration in
eighteen-hundred
and something.

Don't look over your
shoulder, nothing
there. All gone
long time passed
without a backward
glance.

You are the thing
they left behind.

SOUNDS OF A NOVEMBER NIGHT

The clock tocks away
the time as
the roof turbine
makes its
banshee yowl.

November night
is early at the window.
Soft sighs
come with sleep
and snores wake
the living.
Yellow light on the desk
gives word
to the sounds
that live
in this house.

HOT

The wheat is cut
on that 110 degree day.
Warm, brown and gold
we walk the steamy
fry-an-egg sidewalk.

School starts this week.
Heat schedule
till fall sets in.
Too many days

heat the only thing
anyone talks about.
Too hot.
Too hot.

OCEAN WATER SWEAT

The ocean water necessary
to make rain
that will water
Kansas wheat fields,
a billion years gone.
The row crops gone
in the heat.
Dust hangs in
the still air
as the thermometer
breaks meteorologist's charts.
Only sweat
cools the body.

IS THE GRASS GREEN

Landscape changes
wherever you go.
Kansas prairie grass,
horizon and sky.
Colorado mountains
that touch the clouds.
Missouri River bluffs
and forest of trees.
New Mexico mesas,
mountains and cactus.

We change as we roam.
The landscape is out there.

We look and wonder
and then step
into wet morning grass.
Wet shoes walk to
the car and resume
everyday life.
Driving down the street
the landscape constructs
itself around us.

GOLD CORONADO DIDN'T FIND

Down I-135 I drive
by Coronado Heights.
Highest elevation
in ten counties.

Only been there once.
Graffiti mars the
surface and stone
picnic tables
dance around its base.

The land still goes
on to the horizon.
Looking out I imagine
nothing there.
Now the wheat fields
a gold Coronado didn't know.

GATEWAY TO FALL

Sun comes up
bringing with it heat.

Why so hot? I wonder
as my head throbs
from sinus problems,
my perpetual companion.

I long for cool breezes
and weather that
doesn't burn grass
brown and crunchy.

I remember the
month is August.

FUNNY TREES

The one that looks like
it has its hair parted down
the middle like
one of the Three Stooges.

Then there is our tree
a large overgrown
bush with branches
going everywhere.

Character they have
and strength
to stand
the Kansas winds.

FROST PAINTS THE LEAVES

Hard frost
has not come.
The trees are still green
in October
a shade
of dark forest.
Some are starting
to turn a pale yellow.
Frost's finger will touch
as if it were
a paintbrush.
The colors will be
brown
orange
yellow
red.

THE MAXIM WE LIVE BY

The sky over Kansas
tells the weather.
He describes the clouds
as a writer would,
puff ball round
tinged in orange.
The spring sun
is going down
as we turn
into our drive.

Ready to close
everything up,
doors, windows,
early to bed,
the maxim we
live by.

DRY LAND

Irrigation rig
sits rusting
by the river
as it laps the bank.

Water precious
in the dry
prairie grass.

BLUE SPRUCE IN KANSAS

A sea green boat
dry sod setting
in the September sun.
Little pointed needles protect
small squirrels
that play tag
below the hem
of your flaring dress
decoration
in my bay window
at Christmas.
Only now you send
your roots
into the soil.
Not for a saw
or an ornament only
do you stand.

ALL PLANTS NEED WATER

Drought
the land claims,
as the Kansas prairie sun
scorches grass
to a sand yellow.

Rain dribbles down the window,
not watering the green
mother-in-law's tongue that sits
on the opposite side
of the glass.

Dark
scrubby paper leaves
turn upward,
their throats needing
a drink as
the white watering can
pours.

COMING OF THE WINTER SOLSTICE

The airplane plant
on the wire
shelf
next to
the
mother-in-law's tongue
panda's ear
soft and velvety
green
all look out
on dried
sand brown
grass
as the November
sun moves
in the sky
to herald
the solstice.

THINKING OF KIOWA LEGENDS

My mind wanders
and I wonder
about images
of this place
built on
Kiowa legends.

Outside my window
mountains loom.
Hills that look
like a child built them.
Small cubes upon larger ones
stacked and restacked
each upon another.
Wichita Mountains
they are called.
Quartz deposits
and sacred ground
of the Kiowa.

SUN WORSHIPER

Sun outlines
windows from
the southeastern sky.

Its warmth on my back
heats me through,
dissolving the cold
that has settled in
my bones.

I become a
sun worshiper
as the gray days
of winter increase.

A WEED FOR A STATE FLOWER

Sunflowers march
in the ditch
next to the road
yellow faces turned
to the sun.

A weed a symbol
of a state's flatland
going toward the horizon.

POST ROCK COUNTRY

The square yellow blocks
of sandstone create
walls and posts for fences.

Post rock country
they call this place.

An art to making
the posts and bricks.

I watch the man
drill holes in
the rock
placing spikes, hammering—

the split happens.
A long post
halved for
fences.

KNOWING THE WIND

Trees rattle
as wind wipes
branches
shaking dry leaves.

Wind is normal.
Good wind sounds
like the rustle of
taffeta as a bride
walks down a church aisle.

Bad wind
takes you out
on the porch
to watch the sky.
Tornadoes, thunderstorms,
and seventy mile an hour wind
as sirens sound, listen.

GREEN ORANGES

These oranges are green.
Not a true orange—
all knobby. Osage
named for the Indians.
Only good for keeping
moths away.

Driving down country roads
we see
these live green balls,
some still hanging
in the trees.

Put them
in your basement
the old timers say.
Poisonous but useful.

GOING TO NOVEMBER

In October the fans still turn
to the global warming
of a lingering
Kansas summer.

Soon winter will
come coating us
with ice and snow.

Pull down the storm windows.
Put away the lawn mower.
Check the motor
on the snow blower.

Find the boots.
Locate the mittens.
Buy a new coat
for the child grown
too tall
for last year's version.

Only then can October
go to November.

VAGABOND LONGINGS

Driving toward Hays
white birds covering the field
an interruption where
sky and land meet
in the long line
that is stretched like
a rubber band
that might bust.
Never turning back,
only
moving
towards that horizon.

Daughters Taller Than Their Mothers

BUTCHERING

My feet didn't touch
the floor when I sat at the
kitchen table facing the window,
picture frame around
the tree where
the pig hung.

Grandma in the background
turning the grinder
making head cheese, my
father's favorite.

The pig I fed
corn to over the fence
by the barn.
We stomped mud,
spewing it everywhere
running from the pen
to the lilac bush,
Grandma hollering
loud and long
come to supper.

Burn the sausage
please.
The pig
a picture
still in my memory.

SCHOOL IN AUGUST

The wheat is harvested
and still the sun
sends the thermometer
to a hundred and ten.

The dry dirt blows
in the wind as
I drive past the school.

Windows shut
air conditioning blowing
its coolness.

Waiting in the car
for the last daughter.

OUR MOTHER'S DAUGHTER

> "... even as I carry
> the ghost of my mother ..."
> —Maxine Kumin, "The Envelope"

Always her daughter
never do we grow up.
None of us anything but
our mother's daughter.

Look in the mirror and see
her face
woman who bore us.

The ghost we carry
tells us
do better, be better.
Remember who you are.

GROWING THINGS

The classroom science center
overflows with small white foam cups
of brown potting soil.
Each holds a bean seed.
Small hands placed them there
with the hope
each would sprout.

A child holds
a glass,
wet paper towel,
bean seed sandwich.
A sight of awe
in a life
of growing things.

DAUGHTERS TALLER THAN THEIR MOTHER

Thirteen months apart.
July fifth comes
around and a year later
another daughter on
August fourth.

They grow older
and I wonder
at my missing them.

The phone breathes
their voices
and I hang
on the words.

No longer
babes in arms
taller than
their mother
always. ·

THE CAT DEFIES ME

The clink of spoon against
an empty blue glass cereal bowl
in a house inhabited only
by me and a marmalade cat
tells me to holler,

“Get off the table, Mick!”

a chore I do often
when chairs
are not pushed under the table.

It’s an easy jump
for a seventeen pound
yellow cat
that defies me.

THE OLD ONES

We sat on chairs,
in the semi-darkness.
The lath work shelves
glowed in the lantern's light.
The people, who were they?
I don't remember
Great-aunt Jessie.
My grandmother's twin sister,
her husband
the sheriff or was
he someone else?
My mother and my father.
The old ones are
now me.

NOT EQUAL

He is twice my size.
A man bigger than the woman
he calls wife.
I am small.
Most men are bigger
than I am.
One plus one does not equal two.

THE GHOST OF A MEMORY

O'Keeffe returned to Ghost Ranch.
It gave her what she needed.
Eagle Claw and Bean Necklace
Rib and Jawbone
She painted five still lifes,
five flowers, and two
that had bones in them.

I stand in front of the painting
of a Native American dancer
at Quartz Mountain
and remember the trip—
O'Keeffe's Ghost Ranch.
I was to paint.
Then the phone call
that announced my
grandson's death
at nineteen months.
No paint for me.
Bones, no more.

ANTIQUE CRADLE

Sky is always there.
The clouds boil up.

In places full of trees
I get claustrophobic,
closed in when
I can't see the sky.

Ancestor of the women
who traveled by wagon,
who built sod houses
and brought the
cradle my children
slept in.

A DAUGHTER'S MUSIC

The dry brown leaf curls
around the car's radio antenna,
vibrates a rhythm like
the violin strings
she now chooses to play.
Far away in L.A.
learning Persian
and the violin,
her music doesn't
travel to Kansas.

COUNTING PRAYER

Standing in the kitchen
words wash over me
as the sink fills
with soapy water.

Threatening words
pierce as a sewing needle.

My mind's shout
leaps to my closed lips—
only my heart worries
as beads slip
through my fingers
counting prayers.

The Only Life You Could Save

A SMALL WOMAN IN A KANSAS WIND

A bird trying to fly
in a strong wind
rises like an elevator
still flapping it wings.

That's the way I am
moving only in
the direction I'm pushed.
The wind at my back
and no large
Art History book
to hold me down.

WARMING THE BONES OF A SMALL BONED WOMAN

Water boiled for tea.
The essence smells
of strawberries and cinnamon.
Steam rises spreading
the scent.
Hands hold the earth
made mug to warm
the cold from them.
Rubbing the curves,
feeling the rim,
hefting the handle.
A memory of
other caresses
as brown liquid warms.

THIRST QUENCHER

Lemonade yellow seeps
through the translucent
pitcher into a glass.

The tang on my tongue
quenches heat and sweat
reminding me of ice and
cool blue water splashing.

Drinking from the glass
gasping thirst away.

Thirst and longing always
companions
looking for quenching.

FIRST TIME AWAY FROM HOME

You were chartreuse
on the broken cement
sidewalk. I nearly
stepped on you
a young woman
her first time
away from home.

Looking behind me
the green snake
a memory along
with a wish
to change the choices.

THE WORDS GIVEN

> "It is an extremely painful and dangerous way to live – split between a publicly acceptable persona, and a part of yourself that you perceive as the essential, the creative and powerful self . . ."
> — Adrienne Rich, *On Lies, Secrets, and Silence: Selected Prose 1966-1978*

Danger in a life
that is everyday
is a piece of brown
beer bottle glass,
snagged by the tread
of your shoe.

As a split persona
you have walked
the jagged chasm
for years.

The serpent you've created
rises and ties
your tongue
strangling the sound
that trickles past
the gate of your teeth.

Your burden the words
given your daughters.

MAP ON THE THRESHOLD

On the threshold
doors open and close.
the churn of thoughts
scamper like small animals,
leaving invisible tracks
that only nerve endings register.

Take a step forward.
Shoes polished,
handkerchief in the pocket,
never go anywhere
that you don't
wear clean underwear.
Old maxims jump
to fill the mind.

Frost's road not taken
looms in front of me,
but there's no map.

LOOKING FOR A HOME

Cat's yellow eyes pierce
the night.
Dawn edges the
horizon as a squall
taps at my window.
I look.
His gray and white
tabbyness vibrates.
His nose pushes
and spreads on the glass.
Patterns of yellow
from the gold
rug fur feline
who lives here.
Inside he tells me
no not
another cat—
they can't get along.

LISTENING TO THE NIGHT

Listening to the night
rain falls on the grass
outside my window.
Cool air moves past
the slatted blinds
as music
accompanies the
rain drifting down
to sleep in the earth.
I push the covers
back and slip out of
a sleep that
won't come.

HIDING BEHIND WORDS

I'm hearing voices
as I hide behind
the triangular pedestal
of pottery
not wanting to talk
or speak. Oh, I can't.
Words are for
paper only,
silence the
prime mover
punctuated by
the grinding
of the furnace's
warm air.

DRIVE MY EXILE

> "... if you don't honor that impulse, whether it's exile or assimilation, redemption or destruction, revenge or love."
> —Betsy Lerner, *The Forest for the Trees*

All these things
drive my exile.
A combustion engine
at the edge of looking,
the spark of flame
a fuel,
explodes in creation.
I draw
my outline
as the mechanism
pulls me
to its destination.

WE DON'T SPEAK

My mouth sealed
shut.
In the night I sit
waiting for daylight.
Whisper secrets
telling what you
don't want told.
Protection.
The boulder of the
world rolls downhill
too crazy against
the body.
Shockwaves pass
overhead
leaving silent sound
behind them.

WILL I EVER FIT

In the present I sit
in the library
at Quartz Mountain.
The blue dot on my nametag denotes
that I am a part
of a certain group,
that means I belong
now, here in this place.

Going home means
being not of a place, always
even as a child
the last one picked.
I cried myself to sleep.
Belonging's a crucial need,
even at fifty-four.

SUN THROUGH THE EAST WINDOW OF MY OFFICE

Sun's gold outlines my desk
each object set apart.

The fan whirrs above my head
to keep the sun's warmth at bay.

Paper, pen, books the tools
of this gold wood desk.

Sun outlines my reading glasses
with the cord of blue, red and green.

The clay bowl holds silver paper clips
shiny and sparkling in the light.

As my hand writes words
the shadow on the paper repeats.

A MOTHER WAITING IN THE SCHOOL PARKING LOT

The apple tree sits
in an alcove of the building.

Its apples stay
green never
turning red.

I want to get out
of the car
and pick one
to taste
the sweet juice.

Then I remember
where I am.
A principal's face
materializes in my mind.
Schools frown
on vandals.

THE PAIN IS AN ANIMAL

Its eyes are small
bright moons
reflecting light
that scares and alerts
the nerve endings
fight or flight
boils up
as if it were a pot
of soup ready to flood the stove.

Wondering at this animal
inside me I talk to it
in whispers
telling it lies that
I know won't ease its pain.

LOOKING BACK

Looking back
through the door,
wondering
where I want to go.

I step out lost
in furrows
of thought.

Fifty-four summers
and where
have I traveled to?

That road doesn't
take me anywhere.
My mind is lost
in its scrabble game.

Too many words
too many jobs to do
too many, to many.

THE ONLY LIFE YOU COULD SAVE

Thinking on words
my hip hurts.
The flute music
bounds off the walls.
My mind ticks
over the thoughts
coursing through it.
What life I wonder?
A change has
already happened
and I can't
seem to stay with it.

KEEPING TIME

> "Some time is longer that the rest,
> and some is very short,"
> — Emily Dickinson, letter

The year is ending as frost appears
to glaze the cold metal car
like a birthday cake
with too many candles.
Fifty-four years of wanting
and the clock seems
to get louder
with every tick.
With a snap of fingers
I am no longer young
and the clock still
keeps time.

HIGH SCHOOL JUNIOR

You were the smallest
in chemistry class.
Eighty-seven pounds to the football
center's two hundred forty.
You didn't know
that being shy
was not an affliction
that would be with you
all your life.
Believing others
was your downfall.
So now I tell you
it was all right
that you grew into me.

GREET A DAY

I roll over wanting to stay
longer in this cocoon of warmth.
My leg aches a reminder of my fall.
If I stay here I won't be able to walk.
My body does its groaning
getting up ritual.
Each muscle, each bone,
creaking and moving
with fifty-three years worth
of growth, travel
and just living.
They remind me
to keep moving.

THE CURSE

Night closes
around me.

Everyone is in bed
but me.

The only light
a lamp above my shoulders.

The cat purrs
loud as cars pass.

Insomnia the disease
I curse.

My body shakes
its nervous ritual.

SOMEONE CALLS MY NAME

Hear your name
spoken far away
given on the day
of your birth,
so common.

Now you choose
“Walks-in-Strength”
like the Native Americans.

Walks towards,
walks away,
treads a path
that the name
led you to.

Two last names—
one a tribute
to your mother
the other your
husband’s.

NEEDS

Everyone needs:

food, shelter, a good night's
sleep, shoes for feet to
tread cement streets.
A shirt, a coat
to keep out the cold.

Everyone needs:

to see and hear music,
painting, words on a page,
their child's face with a smile
to love and care
to see beauty and peace.

ACKNOWLEDGEMENTS

I want to thank Lori Brack, my editor, for her conscientious work on the book. Thanks to Pam Harris for her wonderful graphic art work. Thanks to Mary Williamson for being a writer friend who listens. Thanks to Anna Shultz for being my first reader. Thanks to the staff at the Salina Public Library for their support. Thanks to Joe McKenzie for his support. Thanks to the Kansas Authors Club for being instrumental in getting me back into writing. Thanks to Jim Riordan and Mary Gaetz for being there at the beginning. Thanks to Ann Lucas for taking my poems to Iran to bridge the cultural gap. Thanks to Jennifer Riordan for being the youngest child and being willing to listen to her mother even when she doesn't want to. Thanks to Bill Riordan, my husband who supports me even when he doesn't know what's going on. Thanks to everyone who helped on this project.

Susan Kinney-Riordan's poetry and short fiction have appeared in Potpourri, Orange Willow Review, Pennsylvania English, Woman of the Plains and RiverSedge. Two of her short plays were produced by the Salina Community Theater. She earned her MA in 2002 from Goddard College in Plainfield, Vermont. Susan works as a library assistant at the Salina Public Library. She is married and lives in Salina, Kansas with her husband and the youngest of their four children.